MW00462523

The Ten Ancient Scrolls For Success

from
The Greatest Salesman in the World

by
Og Mandino

Over 14,000,000 copies in print.

All rights reserved. Published by Frederick Fell Publishing, Inc., 2131 Hollywood Blvd., Hollywood, FL 33020.

Reproduction, translation, or use in any form by any means of any part of this work beyond that permitted by Section 107 or 108 of the 1976 United States Copyright Act without the permission of the copyright owner is unlawful. Requests for permission or further information should be addressed to the Permissions Department, Frederick Fell Publishing, Inc., 2131 Hollywood Boulevard, Hollywood, FL 33020.

This publication is designed to provide accurate and authoritative information in regard to the subject matter covered. It is sold with the understanding that the publisher is not engaged in rendering legal, accounting, or other professional service. If legal advice or other assistance is required, the services of a competent professional person should be sought. *From A Declaration of Principles jointly adopted by a Committee of the American Bar Association and a Committee of Publishers.*

Library of Congress Cataloging-in Publication Data
Mandino, Og
    [Greatest salesman in the world. Selections]
    The ten ancient scrolls for success : from The greatest salesman in the world / by Og Mandino
        p. cm.
    ISBN 0-88391-094-2
    I. Title.
    PS3563.A464G76   1997
    813'.54--dc21   97-8558
                                     CIP

Printed in USA
10 9 8 7 6 5 4 3 2

Design by Chris Hetzer

The text of *The Ten Ancient Scrolls for Success* itself first appeared in *The Greatest Salesman in the World,* by Og Mandino copyright 1996, 1968, published by Lifetime Books, Inc.

The Ten Ancient Scrolls For Success

Fell's

Foreword

Success always leaves clues and the people that find their way on the path to success often do so by following the clues that have been left by other successful people. Unfortunately, only a small percentage of the world's population manage to find the clues that lead to a life filled with success and happiness. Even more regretful is the fact that out of all those who do achieve success, only the compassionate few will take time out and draw a map to help others find their way.

Og Mandino was indeed one of those compassionate few and the Ancient Scrolls are a map unlike any other. Out of his personal search for the answers to life's questions, Og discovered secrets to success revealed by some of the greatest minds our world has ever known. With his unique gift of writing, Og was able to capture these secrets and relate them through the ten ancient scrolls.

The priceless wisdom of the scrolls is like precious jewels which can be used to purchase the greatest riches life has to offer. Each scroll is like a golden key that can unlock the mystery behind ten of the most important issues which confront every human being.

1. Habit
The first scroll reveals how to develop the habits that will guarantee your success. You will discover a secret that has been used by many to destroy bad habits, replace them with good habits, and put you on automatic pilot toward a life filled with happiness.

2. Love
The second scroll will teach you how to maintain the kind of outlook and attitude that will enable you to love others more freely. As a result of applying this one principle you will be amazed at how quickly and abundantly love will come back to you in return.

3. Persistence
The third scroll will show you how to develop a mind set that is immune to the pain of rejection. It will empower you with the ability to penetrate every obstacle and challenge and reach your desired destiny of success.

4. Self-Esteem
The fourth scroll will help you to develop a greater appreciation for who you really are. This enhanced sense of self-worth will also increase the value others place upon you.

5. Time
The fifth scroll enables you to see the element of time from a perspective that will maximize your daily productivity. This scroll will show you how to destroy the regrets of the past and worries about the future, so that you can enjoy your present life to its fullest.

6. Emotions
The sixth scroll teaches you how to control the emotional ups and downs that are a natural part of life. Through this scroll you will also learn how to tolerate and even influence the mood swings in others.

7. Happiness
The seventh scroll will show you how to obtain and maintain the most sought after quality in life — happiness. You will also learn how to multiply your own happiness simply by sharing it with others.

8. Progress
The eighth scroll reveals how you can systematically ensure that you will make constant progress toward your goals. Through this scroll you will discover how to enhance your personal value and increase your ability to perform.

9. Action
The ninth scroll will empower you with a dynamic force

that is the basis of all great achievement — the ability to take action. You shall discover how to overcome your fears and destroy the crippling effects of procrastination.

10. Faith

The tenth scroll reveals how you can tap into the source of infinite power and intelligence. This scroll will equip you with the ability to go far beyond your own human limitations. As a result, you will achieve a level of success that is nothing less than supernatural.

There are some who think of the scrolls as merely an interesting climax to a fictional tale. Yet there are others who realize the scrolls can unlock an unlimited fortune. The proof of the priceless value of the scrolls is evidenced by the real life impact which these magical words have had upon our world.

The Greatest Salesman in the World is still, to this day, the most popular book ever written on the subject of sales. More than any book of its kind, this extraordinary classic has influenced the lives of people all over the world, having been translated into 22 languages and Braille. It is more than mere coincidence that this amazing book about the world's greatest salesman would become the world's greatest selling book of its kind.

Imagine, for just a moment, if God Himself were to reveal the secrets to success within a collection of ancient scrolls? What if the messenger that He gave the scrolls to was instructed to only share the secrets with a specially chosen person? If this were true, the messenger would have been Og Mandino and the chosen person would have been you.

Just as in the story of *The Greatest Salesman in the World*, there is a divine sign that indicates you are indeed that chosen person. It is a glorious star and right now it is shining brightly above your head because of your burning desire to know the secrets to success. It shines with the light of faith because you believe that there are clues that can lead you on the path to a life of fulfillment, joy and happiness. Out of hope, it shines like a beacon leading you to become all that you have ever dreamed. All that remains now is to learn and apply the principles that you will find within *The Ten Ancient Scrolls for Success.*

— **Robert Nelson**
Instructor for The Greatest Sales Training
in the World and Founder of The
Innovation Training Academy

Contents

Introduction

From *The Greatest Salesman in the World*

Hello . . . I am Og Mandino.

Some memories of my long-ago childhood are still very vivid, especially when I think of that special little red-headed Irish lady who was my loving mother. She had a special dream for her son. "Someday," she would tell me, again and again, "someday you will be a writer . . . not just a writer but a *great* writer!"

Well . . . I bought her dream. Most kids resent having their parents plan their future but I liked the idea. A famous writer.

Yes! Mother had me reading grown-up books from the library long before I entered the first grade and I was always writing short stories for her approval.

In my senior year of high school I was editor of the school paper and our plans were that in the fall I would attend the University of Missouri because we believed that they had the best journalism school in the country.

And, then . . . six weeks after I graduated from high school, my mother dropped dead in our kitchen while she was making lunch for me.

I had a terrible time trying to deal with her passing. Instead of going on to college in the fall of 1940, I went to work in a paper factory and, in 1942, I joined the Army Air Corps. In 1943 I received my officer's commission and my silver wings as a bombardier. I was an "officer and a gentleman" two weeks before I could legally vote. I flew thirty bombing missions over Germany in a B-24 Liberator. Jimmy Stewart also flew in the same heavy bombardment group . . . the 445th. Nice man.

I returned to the United States, after the war had ended, and discovered quickly that there wasn't much of an employment market for bombardiers with only a high school education. After many months of unemployment checks and painful searching, I finally secured a job selling life insurance and married the lady I had been dating when I went to war.

The following ten years were a living hell . . . for me, for her, and even for the lovely daughter we had been blessed with. It seemed that no matter how many hours of the day and night I worked, struggling to sell insurance, we drifted deeper and deeper into debt and I began to do what so many frustrated individuals still do today, to hide from their problems.

On the way home, after a long day of sales calls and canvassing for business, I would stop at a barroom for a drink. After all, I deserved it, didn't I, following such a tough day? Well, soon one drink became two, two became four, four became six and finally my wife and daughter, when they could no longer endure my behavior, left me.

The following two years are no more than a hazy memory. I travelled the country in my old Ford, doing any kind of odd jobs in order to earn enough for another bottle of cheap wine and I spent countless drunken nights in gutters, a sorry wretch of a human being, in a living hell.

Then, one cold wintery morning in Cleveland, one I shall never forget, I almost took my life. I had passed the window of a dingy pawn shop and paused when I saw, inside on a shelf, a small handgun. Attached to its barrel was a yellow tag . .

. $29. I reached into my pocket and re-
moved three ten dollar bills . . . all I had in
the world and I thought . . . "There's the
end to all my problems. I'll buy that gun,
get a couple of bullets and take them back
to that dingy room where I'm staying.
Then I'll put the bullets in the gun, put the
gun to my head . . . and pull the trigger . . .
and I'll never have to face thaty miserable
failure in the mirror ever again."

I don't know what happened next. I
joke about it now and say that I was such
a spineless individual at that time that I
couldn't even muster enough courage to do
away with myself. In any event, I didn't
buy that gun. As snow was falling I turned
away from the pawn shop and commenced
walking until I eventually found myself
inside a public library. It was so warm after the outside chills of November.

I began wandering among the thousands of books until I found myself

standing in front of the shelves containing scores of volumes on self-help, success, and motivation. I selected several of them, went to a nearby table and commenced reading, searching for some answers. Where had I gone wrong? Could I make it with just a high school education? Was there any hope for me? What about my drinking problem? Was it too late for me? Was I doomed now to a life of frustration, failure, and tears?

That library visit was the first of many library visits I began making as I wandered across the country, searching for Og Mandino. I must have read hundreds of books dealing with success and gradually my drinking subsided. Then, in a library in Concord, New Hampshire, I discovered W. Clement Stone's great classic, *Success Through a Positive Mental Attitude* . . . and my life has never been the same since then.

I was so impressed with Stone's philosophy of success, that one must be prepared to pay a price in order to achieve any worthwhile goals, that I wanted to work for the man. His book jacket indicated that he was president of Combined Insurance Company of America and I searched until I found a subsidiary of that company in Boston and applied for a salesman's job. At about that same time, I met a lovely lady who had a lot more faith in me than I had in myself and when Mr. Stone's insurance company hired this thirty-two year old loser, I married the lady. Bette and I have now been together for forty years.

Within a year I was promoted to sales manager in the wide-open, and cold, territory of Northern Maine. I hired several young potato farmers, taught them how to sell, applying Stone's philosophy of a positive mental attitude, and we were soon breaking company records.

Then I took a week off from work and rented a typewriter. You see, the dream of writing had *never* really faded from my heart. I wrote a sales manual on how one sells insurance in the rural areas, retyped it as neatly as I could and sent it to Combined Insurance's home office in Chicago . . . just praying that someone there would recognize the great talent they had buried in Northern Maine.

Well, someone did! The next thing I knew, Bette and I and our new young son, Dana, were moving to Chicago, with all our possessions tied to the roof of our car and I was assigned to the sales promotion department, writing company bulletins. At last... I was finally *writing!*

Mr. Stone also published a small house organ titled *Success Unlimited* which was circulated to all his employees and shareholders. I had been working at the home

office for several months and had become a friend of Mr. Stone's when the editor of his magazine retired. I boldly applied
for the position, although I knew nothing
about magazine editing, and he not only
gave me the job but also entrusted me with
a mission.

Og Mandino

Editor's Statement

You are about to read some of the most treasured words ever written. Author Og Mandino, with 18 books published — many of them best-sellers — is the all-time selling inspirational writer, achieving over 36,000,000 copies sold.

Just short of the Bible, arguably no other books have inspired as many people as Og Mandino's. *The New York Times* describes his writings as "lean prose that told simple stories illustrating basic themes on how to live a successful and happy life."

The Greatest Salesman in the World, the number-one-selling motivational and sales book ever produced, has sold 13 million copies. Now available for the first time, is this easy-to-carry pocket gift edition of the *Greatest Salesman's* ten ancient scrolls.

They most certainly will transform your life and help you find true fulfillment.

Digested from *The Greatest Salesman* are the 10 fundamental principles to live by, along with 250 affirmations and guiding points. Mandino has long been recognized as one of the world's leading storytellers and this edition of priceless wisdom is his best work of all.

Many of the scrolls express simple themes, such as "I will greet this day with love in my heart" or "I will live this day as if it is my last." Yet many people fail to put these scrolls into effect.

Sometimes all we need is a reassuring voice to guide us through the complex maze we have woven for our lives. This book can be read in one sitting but should be studied for hours and practiced for years. It represents the voice of reason, the voice of inspiration, the voice of strength. It will become your voice for a lifetime.

Indeed, this wonderful book is a tribute to Og Mandino, who other than popes and presidents, has moved more people to take positive empowering action than anyone this century.

He pioneered the inspirational field of writing, leading the way for best-selling writers like Zig Ziglar and Anthony Robbins. Mandino appeared on over 1,000 radio and television shows. Once one of the most sought after speakers in the country, he received the highest award (CPAE) given by the National Speakers Association. Listed in Who's Who in the World, he was the first to receive the Napoleon Hill Gold Medal and is a member of the International Speakers Hall of Fame.

Lifetime Books is pleased to be a part of your personal growth and we thank you for reading THE TEN ANCIENT SCROLLS.

— Brian Feinblum
   Senior Editor

Other Books & Audio by Og Mandino

The Greatest Salesman in the World

The Greatest Miracle in the World

The Greatest Secret in the World

The Greatest Gift in the World

The God Memorandum

Og Mandino's Great Trilogy

AUDIO

The Greatest Salesman in the World

The Greatest Miracle in the World

The Greatest Secret in the World

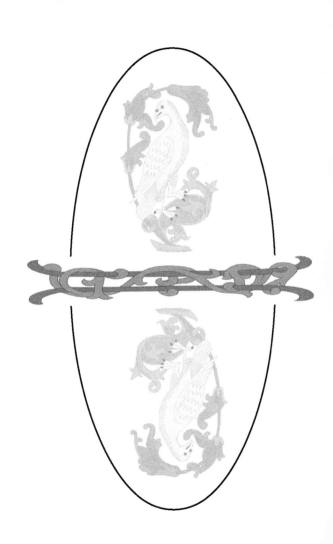

The Scroll Marked

I

*T*oday I begin a new life. Today I shed my old skin which hath too long suffered the bruises of failure and the wounds of mediocrity.

Today I am born anew and my birthplace is a vineyard where there is fruit for all.

Today I will pluck grapes of wisdom from the tallest and fullest vines in the vineyard, for these were planted by the wisest of my profession who have come before me, generation upon generation.

Today I will savor the taste of grapes from these vines and verily I will swallow the seed of success buried in each and new life will sprout within me.

The career I have chosen is laden with opportunity yet it is fraught with heartbreak and despair and the bodies of those who have failed, were they piled one atop another, would cast its shadow down upon all the pyramids of the earth.

Yet I will not fail, as the others, for in my hands I now hold the charts which will guide me through perilous waters to shores which only yesterday seemed but a dream.

Failure no longer will be my payment for struggle. Just as nature made no provision for my body to tolerate pain neither has it made any provision for my life to suffer failure. Failure, like pain, is alien to my life. In the past I accepted it as I accepted pain. Now I reject it and I am prepared for wisdom and principles which will guide me out of the shadows into the sunlight of wealth, position, and happiness far beyond my most extravagant dreams until even the golden apples in the Garden of Hesperides will seem no more than my just reward.

Time teaches all things to he who lives forever but I have not the luxury of eternity. Yet, within my allotted time I must practice the art of patience for nature acts never in haste. To create the olive, king of all trees, a hundred years is required. An onion plant is old in nine weeks. I have lived as an onion plant. It has not pleased me. Now I wouldst become the greatest of olive trees and, in truth, the greatest of salesmen.

And how will this be accomplished? For I have neither the knowledge nor the experience to achieve greatness and already I have stumbled in ignorance and fallen into pools of self-pity. The answer is simple. I will commence my journey unencumbered with either the weight of unnecessary knowledge or the handicap of meaningless experience. Nature already has supplied me with knowledge and instinct far greater than any beast in the forest and the value of experience is overrated, usually by old men who nod wisely and speak stupidly.

In truth, experience teaches thoroughly yet her course of instruction devours men's years so the value of her lessons diminishes with the time necessary to acquire her special wisdom. The end finds it wasted on dead men. Furthermore, experience is comparable to fashion; an action that proved successful today will be unworkable and impractical tomorrow.

Only principles endure and these I now possess, for the laws that will lead me to greatness are contained in the words of these scrolls. What they will teach me is more to prevent failure than to gain success, for what is success other than a state of mind? Which two, among a thousand wise men, will define success in the same words; yet failure is always described but one way. *Failure is man's inability to reach his goals in life, whatever they may be.*

In truth, the only difference between those who have failed and those who have succeeded lies in the difference of their habits. Good habits are the key to all success. Bad habits are the unlocked door to failure. Thus, the first law I will obey, which precedeth all others is — *I will form good habits and become their slaves.*

As a child I was slave to my impulses; now I am slave to my habits, as are all grown men. I have surrendered my free will to the years of accumulated habits and the past deeds of my life have already marked out a path which threatens to imprison my future. My actions are ruled by appetite, passion, prejudice, greed, love, fear, environment, habit, and the worst of these tyrants is habit. Therefore, if I must be a slave to habit let me be a slave to good habits. My bad habits must be destroyed and new furrows prepared for good seed.

I will form good habits and become their slave.

And how will I accomplish this difficult feat? Through these scrolls, it will be done, for each scroll contains a principle which will drive a bad habit from my life and re-

place it with one which will bring me
closer to success. For it is another of
nature's laws that only a habit can
subdue another habit. So, in order for these
written words to perform their chosen task, I
must discipline myself with the first of my new
habits which is as follows:

I will read each scroll for thirty days
in this prescribed manner, before I proceed
to the next scroll.

First, I will read the words in silence
when I arise. Then, I will read the words in
silence after I have partaken of my middday
meal. Last, I will read the words again just
before I retire at day's end, and most important, on this occasion I will read the
words aloud.

On the next day I will repeat this procedure, and I will continue in like manner for
thirty days. Then, I will turn to the next

 scroll and repeat this procedure for another thirty days. I will continue in this manner until I have lived with each scroll for thirty days and my reading has become habit.

And what will be accomplished with this habit? Herein lies the hidden secret of all man's accomplishments. As I repeat the words daily they will soon become a part of my active mind, but more important, they will also seep into my other mind, that mysterious source which never sleeps, which creates my dreams, and often makes me act in ways I do not comprehend.

As the words of these scrolls are consumed by my mysterious mind I will begin to awake, each morning, with a vitality I have never known before. My vigor will increase, my enthusiasm will rise, my desire to meet the world will overcome every fear I once knew at sunrise, and I will be happier than I ever believed it possible to be in this world of strife and sorrow.

Eventually I will find myself reacting to all situations which confront me as I was commanded in the scrolls to react, and soon these actions and reactions will become easy to perform, for any act with practice becomes easy.

Thus a new and good habit is born, for when an act becomes easy through constant repetition it becomes a pleasure to perform and if it is a pleasure to perform it is man's nature to perform it often. When I perform it often it becomes a habit and I become its slave and since it is a good habit this is my will.

Today I begin a new life.

And I make a solemn oath to myself that nothing will retard my new life's growth. I will

  lose not a day from these readings for that day cannot be retrieved nor can I substitute another for it. I must not, I will not, break this habit of daily reading from these scrolls and, in truth, the few moments spent each day on this new habit are but a small price to pay for the happiness and success that will be mine.

As I read and re-read the words in the scrolls to follow, never will I allow the brevity of each scroll nor the simplicity of its words to cause me to treat the scroll's message lightly. Thousands of grapes are pressed to fill one jar with wine, and the grapeskin and pulp are tossed to the birds. So it is with these grapes of wisdom from the ages. Much has been filtered and tossed to the wind. Only the pure truth lies distilled in the words to come. I will drink as instructed and spill not a drop. And the seed of success I will swallow.

Today my old skin has become dust. I will walk tall among men and they will know me not, for today I am a new man, with a new life.

The Scroll Marked II

I will greet this day with love in my heart.

For this is the greatest secret of success in all ventures. Muscle can split a shield and even destroy life but only the unseen power of love can open the hearts of men and until I master this art I will remain no more than a peddler in the market place. I will make love my greatest weapon and none on whom I call can defend against its force.

My reasoning they may counter; my speech they may distrust; my apparel they may disapprove; my face they may reject; and even my bargains may cause them suspicion; yet my love will melt all hearts liken to the sun whose rays soften the coldest clay.

I will greet this day with love in my heart.

And how will I do this? Henceforth will I look on all things with love and I will be born again. I will love the sun for it warms my bones; yet I will love the rain for it cleanses my spirit. I will love the light for it shows me the way; yet I will love the darkness for it shows me the stars. I will welcome happiness for it enlarges my heart; yet I will endure sadness for it opens my soul.

I will acknowledge rewards for they are my due; yet I will welcome obstacles for they are my challenge.

I will greet this day with love in my heart.

And how will I speak? I will laud mine enemies and they will become friends; I will encourage my friends and they will become brothers. Always will I dig for reasons to applaud; never will I scratch for excuses to gossip. When I am tempted to criticize I will bite my tongue; when I am moved to praise I will shout from the roofs.

Is it not so that birds, the wind, the sea and all nature speaks with the music of praise for their creator? Cannot I speak with the same music to his children? Henceforth will I remember this secret and it will challenge my life.

I will greet this day with love
in my heart.

And how will I act? I will love all manners of men for each has qualities to be admired even though they be hidden. With love I will tear down the wall of suspicion and hate which they have built round their hearts and in its place will I build bridges so that my love may enter their souls.

I will love the ambitious for they can inspire me; I will love the failures for they can teach me. I will love the kings for they are but human; I will love the meek for they are divine. I will love the rich for they are yet lonely; I will love the poor for they are so many. I will love the young for the faith they hold; I will love the old for the wisdom

they share. I will love the beauti-
ful for their eyes of sadness; I will
love the ugly for their souls of
peace.

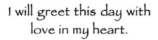

I will greet this day with
love in my heart.

But how will I react to the actions of others? With love. For just as love is my
weapon to open the hearts of men, love is
also my shield to repulse the arrows of hate
and the spears of anger. Adversity and dis-
couragement will beat against my new
shield and become as the softest of rains.
My shield will protect me in the market
place and sustain me when I am alone. It
will uplift me in moments of despair yet it
will calm me in time of exultation. It will
become stronger and more protective with
use until one day I will cast it aside and walk
unencumbered among all manners of men and,

when I do, my name will be raised high on the pyramid of life.

I will greet this day with love in my heart.

And how will I confront each whom I meet? In only one way. In silence and to myself I will address him and say I Love You. Though spoken in silence these words will shine in my eyes, unwrinkle my brow, bring a smile to my lips, and echo in my voice; and his heart will be opened. And who is there who will say nay to my goods when his heart feels my love?

I will greet this day with love in my heart.

And most of all I will love myself. For when I do I will zealously inspect all things which enter my body, my mind, my soul, and my heart. Never will I overindulge the requests of my flesh, rather I will cherish my body with cleanliness and moderation. Never will I allow my mind to be attracted to evil and despair, rather I will uplift it with the knowledge and wisdom of the ages. Never will I allow my soul to become complacent and satisfied, rather I will feed it with meditation and prayer. Never will I allow my heart to become small and bitter, rather I will share it and it will grow and warm the earth.

I will greet this day with love in my heart.

Henceforce will I love all mankind. From this moment all hate is let from my veins for I have not time to hate, only time to love. From this moment I take the first step required to become a man among men. With love I will increase my sales a hundredfold and become a great salesman. If I have no other qualities I can succeed with love alone. Without it I will fail though I possess all the knowledge and skills of the world.

I will greet this day with love,
and I will succeed.

The Scroll Marked

III

I will persist until I succeed.

In the Orient young bulls are tested for the fight arena in a certain manner. Each is brought to the ring and allowed to attack a picador who pricks them with a lance. The bravery of each bull is then rated with care according to the number of times he demonstrates his willingness to charge in spite of the sting of the blade. Henceforth will I recognize that each day I am tested by life in like manner. If I persist, if I continue to try, if I continue to charge forward, I will succeed.

I will persist until I succeed.

I was not delivered unto this world in defeat, nor does failure course in my veins. I am not a sheep waiting to be prodded by my shepherd. I am a lion and I refuse to talk, to walk, to sleep with the sheep. I will hear not those who weep and complain, for their disease is contagious. Let them join the sheep. The slaughterhouse of failure is not my destiny.

I will persist until I succeed.

The prizes of life are at the end of each journey, not near the beginning; and it is not given to me to know how many steps are necessary in order to reach my goal. Failure I may still encounter at the thousandth step, yet success hides behind the next bend in the road. Never will I know how close it lies unless I turn the corner.

Always will I take another step. If that is of no avail I will take another, and yet another. In truth, one step at a time is not too difficult.

I will persist until I succeed.

Henceforth, I will consider each day's effort as but one blow of my blade against a mighty oak. The first blow may cause not a tremor in the wood, nor the second, nor the third. Each blow, of itself, may be trifling, and seem of no consequence. Yet from childish swipes the oak will eventually tumble. So it will be with my efforts of today.

I will be liken to the rain drop which washes away the mountain; the ant who devours a tiger; the star which brightens the earth; the slave who builds a pyramid. I will build my castle one brick at a time for I know that small attempts, repeated, will complete any undertaking.

I will persist until I succeed.

I will never consider defeat and I will remove from my vocabulary such words and phrases as quit, cannot, unable, impossible, out of the question, improbable, failure, unworkable, hopeless, and retreat; for they are the words of fools. I will avoid despair but if this disease of the mind should infect me then I will work on in despair. I will toil and I will endure. I will ignore the obstacles at my feet and keep mine eyes on the goals above my head, for I know that

where dry desert ends, green grass
grows.

I will persist until I succeed.

I will remember the ancient law of averages and I will bend it to my good. I will
persist with knowledge that each failure to
sell will increase my chance for success at
the next attempt. Each nay I hear will bring
me closer to the sound of yea. Each frown
I meet only prepares me for the smile to
come. Each misfortune I encounter will
carry in it the seed of tomorrow's good luck.
I must have the night to appreciate the day.
I must fail often to succeed only once.

I will persist until I succeed.

I will try, and try, and try again. Each
obstacle I will consider as a mere detour to
my goal and a challenge to my profession. I

will persist and develop my skills as the mariner develops his, by learning to ride out the wrath of each storm.

I will persist until I succeed.

Henceforth, I will learn and apply another secret of those who excel in my work. When each day is ended, not regarding whether it has been a success or failure, I will attempt to achieve one more sale. When my thoughts beckon my tired body homeward I will resist the temptation to depart. I will try again. I will make one more attempt to close with victory, and if that fails I will make another. Never will I allow any day to end with a failure. Thus will I plant the seed of tomorrow's success and gain an insurmountable advantage over those who cease their labor at a prescribed time. When others cease their struggle, then mine will begin, and my harvest will be full.

I will persist until I succeed.

Nor will I allow yesterday's success to lull into today's complacency, for this is the great foundation of failure. I will forget the happenings of the day that is gone, whether they were good or bad, and greet the new sun with confidence that this will be the best day of my life.

So long as there is breath in me, that long will I persist. For now I know one of the greatest principles of success; if I persist long enough I will win.

I will persist.
I will win.

The Scroll Marked IV

I am nature's greatest miracle.

Since the beginning of time never has there been another with my mind, my heart, my eyes, my ears, my hands, my hair, my mouth. None that came before, none that live today, and none that come tomorrow can walk and talk and move and think exactly like me. All men are my brothers yet I am different from each. I am a unique creature.

I am nature's greatest miracle.

Although I am of the animal kingdom, animal rewards alone will not satisfy me. Within me burns a flame which has been passed from generations uncounted and its heat is a constant irritation to my spirit to become better than I am, and I will. I will fan this flame of dissatisfaction and proclaim my uniqueness to the world.

None can duplicate my brush strokes, none can make my chisel marks, none can duplicate my handwriting, none can produce my child, and, in truth, none has the ability to sell exactly as I. Henceforth, I will capitalize on this difference for it is an asset to be promoted to the fullest.

I am nature's greatest miracle.

Vain attempts to imitate others no longer will I make. Instead will I place my uniqueness on display in the market place. I will proclaim it, yea, I will sell it. I will begin now to accent my differences; hide my similarities. So too will I apply this principle to the goods I sell. Salesman and goods, different from all others, and proud of the difference.

I am a unique creature of nature.

I am rare, and there is value in all rarity; therefore, I am valuable. I am the end product of thousands of years of evolution; therefore, I am better equipped in both mind and body than all emperors and wisemen who preceded me.

But my skills, my mind, my heart, and my body will stagnate, rot, and die lest I put them to good use. I have unlimited potential. Only a small portion of my brain do I employ; only a paltry amount of my muscles do I flex. A hundredfold or more can I increase my accomplishments of yesterday and this I will do, beginning today.

Nevermore will I be satisfied with yesterday's accomplishments nor will I indulge, anymore, in self-praise for deeds which in reality are too small to even acknowledge. I can accomplish far more than I have, and I will, for why should the miracle which produced me end with my birth? Why can I not extend that miracle to my deeds of today?

I am nature's greatest miracle.

I am not on this earth by chance. I am here for a purpose and that purpose is to grow into a mountain, not to shrink to a grain of sand. Henceforth will I apply all my efforts to become the highest mountain of all and I will strain my potential until it cries for mercy.

I will increase my knowledge of mankind, myself, and the goods I sell, thus my sales will multiply.

I will practice, and improve, and polish the words I utter to sell my goods, for this is the foundation on which I will build my career and never will I forget that many have attained great wealth and success with only one sales talk, delivered with excellence. Also will I seek constantly to improve my manners and graces, for they are the sugar to which are all attracted.

I am nature's greatest miracle.

I will concentrate my energy on the challenge of the moment and my actions will help me forget all else. The problems of my home will be left in my home. I will think naught of my family when I am in the market place for this will cloud my thoughts. So too will the problems of the market place be left in the market place and I will think naught of my profession when I am in my home for this will dampen my love.

There is no room in the market place for my family, nor is there room in my home for the market. Each I will divorce from the other and thus will I remain wedded to both. Separate must they remain or my career will die. This is a paradox of the ages.

I am nature's greatest miracle.

I have been given eyes to see and a mind to think and now I know a great secret of life for I perceive, at last, that all my problems, discouragements, and heartaches are, in truth, great opportunities in disguise. I will no longer be fooled by the garments they wear for mine eyes are open. I will look beyond the cloth and I will not be deceived.

I am nature's greatest miracle.

No beast, no plant, no wind, no rain, no rock, no lake had the same beginning as I, for I was conceived in love and brought forth with a purpose. In the past I have not considered this fact but it will henceforth shape and guide my life.

I am nature's greatest miracle.

And nature knows not defeat. Eventually, she emerges victorious and so will I, and with each victory the next struggle becomes less difficult. I will win, and I will become a great salesman, for I am unique.

I am nature's greatest miracle.

The Scroll Marked V

I will live this day as if it is my last. And what shall I do with this last precious day which remains in my keeping? First, I will seal up its container of life so that not one drop spills itself upon the sand. I will waste not a moment mourning yesterday's misfortunes, yesterday's defeats, yesterday's aches of the heart, for why should I throw good after bad?

Can sand flow upward in the hour glass? Will the sun rise where it sets and set where it rises? Can I relive the errors of yesterday and right them? Can I call back yesterday's wounds and make them whole? Can I become younger than yesterday? Can I take back the evil that was spoken, the blows that were struck, the pain that was caused? No. Yesterday is buried forever and I will think of it no more.

I will live this day as if it is my last.

And what then shall I do? Forgetting yesterday neither will I think of tomorrow. Why should I throw **now** after **maybe**? Can tomorrow's sand flow through the glass before today's? Will the sun rise twice this morning? Can I perform tomorrow's deeds while standing in today's path? Can I place tomorrow's gold in today's purse? Can tomorrow's child be born today? Can tomorrow's death cast its shadow backward and darken today's joy? Should I concern myself over events which I may never witness? Should I torment myself with problems that may never come to pass? No! Tomorrow lies buried with yesterday, and I will think of it no more.

I will live this day as if it is my last.

This day is all I have and these hours are now my eternity. I greet this sunrise with cries of joy as a prisoner who is reprieved from death. I lift mine arms with thanks for this priceless gift of a new day. So too, I will beat upon my heart with gratitude as I consider all who greeted yesterday's sunrise who are no longer with the living today. I am indeed a fortunate man and today's hours are but a bonus, undeserved.

Why have I been allowed to live this extra day when others, far better than I, have departed? Is it that they have accomplished their purpose while mine is yet to be achieved? Is this another opportunity for me to become the man I know I can be? Is there a purpose in nature? Is this my day to excel?

I will live this day as if it is my last.

I have but one life and life is naught but a measurement of time. When I waste one I destroy the other. If I waste today I destroy the last page of my life. Therefore, each hour of this day will I cherish for it can never return. It cannot be banked today to be withdrawn on the morrow, for who can trap the wind? Each minute of this day will I grasp with both hands and fondle with love for its value is beyond price. What dying man can purchase another breath though he willingly give all his gold? What price dare I place on the hours ahead? I will make them priceless!

I will live this day as if it is my last.

I will avoid with fury the killers of time. Procrastination I will destroy with action; doubt I will bury under faith; fear I will dismember with confidence.

Where there are idle mouths I will listen not; where there are idle bodies I will visit not. Henceforth I know that to court idleness is to steal food, clothing, and warmth from those I love. I am not a thief. I am a man of love and today is my last chance to prove my love and my greatness.

I will live this day as if it is my last.

The duties of today I shall fulfill today. Today I shall fondle my children while they are young; tomorrow they will be gone, and so will I. Today I shall embrace my woman with sweet kisses; tomorrow she will be gone, and so will I. Today I shall lift up a friend in need; tomorrow he will no longer cry for help, nor will I hear his cries. Today I shall give myself in sacrifice and work; tomorrow I will have nothing to give, and there will be none to receive.

I will live this day as if it is my last.

And if it is my last, it will be my greatest monument. This day I will make the best day of my life. This day I will drink every minute to its full. I will savor its taste and give thanks. I will maketh every hour count and each minute I will trade only for something of value. I will labor harder than ever before and push my muscles until they cry for relief,

and then I will continue. I will make
more calls than ever before. I will
sell more goods than ever before. I

will earn more gold than ever before. Each
minute of today will be more fruitful than hours
of yesterday. My last must be my best.

I will live this day as if it is my last.

And if it is not, I shall fall to my knees
and give thanks.

The Scroll Marked VI

*T*oday I will be master of my emotions. The tides advance; the tides recede. Winter goes and summer comes. Summer wanes and the cold increases. The sun rises; the sun sets. The moon is full; the moon is black. The birds arrive; the birds depart. Flowers bloom; flowers fade. Seeds are sown; harvests are reaped. All nature is a circle of moods and

I am a part of nature and so, like the tides, my moods will rise; my moods will fall.

Today I will be master of my emotions.

It is one of nature's tricks, little understood, that each day I awaken with moods that have changed from yesterday. Yesterday's joy will become today's sadness; yet today's sadness will grow into tomorrow's joy. Inside me is a wheel, constantly turning from sadness to joy, from exultation to depression, from happiness to melancholy. Like the flowers, today's full bloom of joy will fade and wither into despondency, yet I will remember that as today's dead flower carries the seed of tomorrow's bloom so, too, does today's sadness carry the seed of tomorrow's joy.

Today I will be master of my emotions.

And how will I master these emotions so that each day will be productive? For unless my mood is right the day will be a failure. Trees and plants depend on the weather to flourish but I make my own weather, yea I transport it with me.

If I bring rain and gloom and darkness and pessimism to my customers then they will react with rain and gloom and darkness and pessimism and they will purchase naught. If I bring joy and enthusiasm and brightness and laughter to my customers they will react with joy and enthusiasm and brightness and laughter and my weather will produce a harvest of sales and a granary of gold for me.

Today I will be master of my emotions.

And how will I master my emotions so that every day is a happy day, and a productive one? I will learn this secret of the ages: *Weak is he who permits his thoughts to control his actions; strong is he who forces his actions to control his thoughts.* Each day, when I awake, I will follow this plan of battle before I am captured by the forces of sadness, self-pity and failure—

- *If I feel depressed I will sing.*
- *If I feel sad I will laugh.*
- *If I feel ill I will double my labor.*
- *If I feel fear I will plunge ahead.*
- *If I feel inferior I will wear new garments.*
- *If I feel uncertain I will raise my voice.*
- *If I feel poverty I will think of wealth to come.*
- *If I feel incompetent I will remember past success.*
- *If I feel insignificant I will remember my goals.*

Today I will be master of my emotions.

Henceforth, I will know that only those with inferior ability can always be at their best, and I am not inferior. There will be days when I must constantly struggle against forces which would tear me down. Those such as despair and sadness are simple to recognize but there are others which approach with a smile and the hand of friendship and they can also destroy me. Against them, too, I must never relinquish control—

- *If I become overconfident I will recall my failures.*
- *If I overindulge I will think of past hungers.*
- *If I feel complacency I will remember my competition.*
- *If I enjoy moments of greatness I will remember moments of shame.*

- *If I feel all-powerful I will try to stop the wind.*
- *If I attain great wealth I will remember one unfed mouth.*
- *If I become overly proud I will remember a moment of weakness.*
- *If I feel my skill is unmatched I will look at the stars.*
- *Today I will be master of my emotions.*

A nd with this new knowledge I will also understand and recognize the moods of he on whom I call. I will make allowances for his anger and irritation of today for he knows not the secret of controlling his mind. I can withstand his arrows and insults for now I know that tomorrow he will change and be a joy to approach.

No longer will I judge a man on one meeting; no longer will I fail to call again tomorrow on he who meets me with hate today. This day he will not buy gold chariots for a penny, yet tomorrow he would exchange his home for a tree. My knowledge of this secret will be my key to great wealth.

Today I will be master of my emotions.

Henceforth I will recognize and identify the mystery of moods in all mankind, and in me. From this moment I am prepared to control whatever personality awakes in me each day. I will master my moods through positive action and when I master my moods I will control my destiny.

Today I control my destiny, and my destiny is to become the greatest salesman in the world!

I will become master of myself.
I will become great.

The Scroll Marked VII

I will laugh at the world. No living creature can laugh except man. Trees may bleed when they are wounded, and beasts in the field will cry in pain and hunger, yet only I have the gift of laughter and it is mine to use whenever I choose. Henceforth I will cultivate the habit of laughter.

I will smile and my digestion will improve; I will chuckle and my burdens will be lightened; I will laugh and my life will be lengthened for this is the great secret of long life and now it is mine.

I will laugh at the world.

And most of all, I will laugh at myself for man is most comical when he takes himself too seriously. Never will I fall into this trap of the mind. For though I be nature's greatest miracle am I not still a mere grain tossed about by the winds of time? Do I truly know whence I came or whither I am bound? Will my concern for this day not seem foolish ten years hence? Why should I permit the petty happenings of today to disturb me? What can take place before this sun sets which will not seem insignificant in the river of the centuries?

I will laugh at the world.

And how can I laugh when confronted with man or deed which offends me so as to bring forth my tears or my curses? Four words I will train myself to say until they become a habit so strong that immediately they will appear in my mind whenever good humor threatens to depart from me. These words, passed down from the ancients, will carry me through every adversity and maintain my life in balance. These four words are: *This too shall pass.*

I will laugh at the world.

For all worldly things shall indeed pass. When I am heavy with heartache I shall console myself that this too shall pass; when I am puffed with success I shall warn myself that this too shall pass. When I am strangled in poverty I shall tell myself that this too shall pass; when I am burdened with wealth I shall tell myself that this too shall pass. Yea, verily, where is he who built the pyramid? Is he not buried within its stone? And will the pyramid, one day, not also be buried under sand? If all things shall pass why should I be of concern for today?

I will laugh at the world.

I will paint this day with laughter; I will frame this night in song. Never will I labor to be happy; rather I will remain to busy to be sad. I will enjoy today's happiness today. It is not grain to be stored in a box. It is not wine to be saved in a jar. It cannot be saved for the morrow. It must be sown and reaped on the same day and this I will do, henceforth.

I will laugh at the world.

And with my laughter all things will be reduced to their proper size. I will laugh at my failures and they will vanish in clouds of new dreams; I will laugh at my successes and they will shrink to their true value. I will laugh at evil and it will die untasted; I will laugh at goodness and it will thrive and abound. Each day will be triumphant only when my smiles bring forth smiles from others and this I do in selfishness, for those on whom I frown are those who purchase not my goods.

I will laugh at the world.

Henceforth will I shed only tears of sweat, for those of sadness or remorse or frustration are of no value in the market place whilst each smile can be exchanged for gold and each kind word, spoken from my heart, can build a castle.

Never will I allow myself to become so important, so wise, so dignified, so powerful, that I forget how to laugh at myself and my world. In this matter I will always remain as a child, for only as a child am I given the ability to look up to others; and so long as I look up to another I will never grow to long for my cot.

I will laugh at the world.

And so long as I can laugh never will I be poor. This then, is one of nature's greatest gifts, and I will waste it no more. Only with laughter and happiness can I truly become a success. Only with laughter and happiness can I enjoy the fruits of my labor.

Were it not so, far better would it be to fail, for happiness is the wine that sharpens the taste of the meal. To enjoy success I must have happiness, and laughter will be the maiden who serves me.

I will be happy.
I will be successful.

I will be the greatest salesman the
world has ever known.

The Scroll Marked VIII

*T*oday I will multiply my value a hundredfold.

A mulberry leaf touched with the genius of man becomes silk.

A field of clay touched with the genius of man becomes a castle.

A cyprus tree touched with the genius of man becomes a shrine.

A cut of sheep's hair touched with the genius of man becomes raiment for a king.

If it is possible for leaves and clay and wood and hair to have their value multiplied a hundred, yea a thousand-fold by man, cannot I do the same with the clay which bears my name?

Today I will multiply my value a hundredfold.

I am liken to a grain of wheat which faces one of three futures. The wheat can be placed in a sack and dumped in a stall until it is fed to swine. Or it can be ground to flour and made into bread. Or it can be placed in the earth and allowed to grow until its golden head divides and produces a thousand grains from the one.

I am liken to a grain of wheat with one difference. The wheat cannot choose whether it be fed to swine, ground for bread, or planted to multiply. I have a choice and I will not let my life be fed to swine nor will I let it be ground under the rocks of failure and despair to be broken open and devoured by the will of others.

Today I will multiply my value a hundredfold.

To grow and multiply it is necessary to plant the wheat grain in the darkness of the earth and my failures, my despairs, my ignorance, and my inabilities are the darkness in which I have been planted in order to ripen.

Now, like the wheat grain which will sprout and blossom only if it is nurtured with rain and sun and warm winds, I too must nurture my body and mind to fulfill my dreams. But to grow to full stature the wheat must wait on the whims of nature. I need not wait for I have the power to choose my own destiny.

Today I will multiply my value a hundredfold.

And how will I accomplish this? First I will set goals for the day, the week, the month, the year, and my life. Just as the rain must fall before the wheat will crack its shell and sprout, so must I have objectives before my life will crystallize. In setting my goals I will consider my best performance of the past and multiply it a hundredfold. This will be the standard by which I will live in the future. Never will I be of concern that my goals are too high for is it not better to aim my spear at the moon and strike only an eagle than to aim my spear at the eagle and strike only a rock?

Today I will multiply my value
a hundredfold.

The height of my goals will not
hold me in awe though I may stumble often before they are reached. If I stumble I will rise
and my falls will not concern me for all men
must stumble often to reach the hearth.
Only a worm is free from the worry of stum-
bling. I am not a worm. I am not an onion
plant. I am not a sheep. I am a man. Let
others build a cave with their clay. I will
build a castle with mine.

Today I will multiply my value a hundredfold.

And just as the sun must warm the earth
to bring forth the seedling of wheat so, too,
will the words on these scrolls warm my life
and turn my dreams into reality. Today I
will surpass every action which I performed

yesterday. I will climb today's mountain to the utmost of my ability yet tomorrow I will climb higher than today, and the next will be higher than tomorrow. To surpass the deeds of others is unimportant; to surpass my own deeds is all.

Today I will multiply my value a hundredfold.

And just as the warm wind guides the wheat to maturity, the same winds will carry my voice to those who will listen and my words will announce my goals. Once spoken I dare not recall them lest I lose face. I will be as my own prophet and though all may laugh at my utterances they will hear my plans, they will know my dreams; and thus there will be no escape for me until my words become accomplish deeds.

Today I will multiply my value a hundredfold.

I will commit not the terrible crime of aiming too low.

I will do the work that a failure will not do.

I will always let my reach exceed my grasp.

I will never be content with my performance in the market.

I will always raise my goals as soon as they are attained.

I will always strive to make the next hour better than this one.

I will always announce my goals to the world.

Yet, never will I proclaim my accomplishments. Let the world, instead, approach me with praise and may I have the wisdom to receive it in humility.

Today I will multiply my value a hundredfold.

One grain of wheat when multiplied a hundredfold will produce a hundred stalks.

 Multiply these a hundredfold, ten times, and they will feed all the cities of the earth. Am I not more than a grain of wheat?

Today I will multiply my value a hundredfold.

And when it is done I will do it again, and again, and there will be astonishment and wonder at my greatness as the words of these scrolls are fulfilled in me.

The Scroll Marked IX

*M*y dreams are worthless, my plans are dust, my goals are impossible. All are of no value unless they are followed by action.

I will act now.

Never has there been a map, however carefully executed to detail and scale, which carried its owner over even one inch of ground. Never has there been a parchment of law, however fair, which prevented one crime. Never has there been a scroll, even such as the one that I hold, which earned so much as a penny or produced a single word of acclamation. Action, alone, is the tinder which ignites the map, the parchment, this scroll, my dreams, my plans, my goals, into a living force. Action is the food and drink which will nourish my success.

I will act now.

My procrastination which has held me back was born of fear and now I recognize this secret mined from the depths of all courageous hearts. Now I know that to conquer fear I must always act without hesitation and the flutters in my heart will vanish. Now I know that action reduces the lion of terror to an ant of equanimity.

I will act now.

Henceforth, I will remember the lesson of the firefly who gives off its light only when it is on the wing, only when it is in action. I will become a firefly and even in the day my glow will be seen in spite of the sun. Let others be as butterflies who preen their wings yet depend on the charity of a flower for life. I will be as the firefly and my light will brighten the world.

I will act now.

I will not avoid the tasks of today and charge them to tomorrow for I know that tomorrow never comes. Let me act now even though my actions may not bring happiness or success for it is better to act and fail than not to act and flounder. Happiness, in truth, may not be the fruit plucked by my action yet without action all fruit will die on the vine.

I will act now.

I will act now. I will act now. I will act now. Henceforth, I will repeat these words again and again and again, each hour, each day, every day, until the words became as much a habit as my breathing and the actions which follow become as instinctive as the blinking of my eyelids. With these words I can condition my mind to perform every act necessary for my success. With these words I can condition my mind to meet every challenge which the failure avoids.

I will act now.

I will repeat these words again and again and again. When I awake I will say them and leap from my cot while the failure sleeps yet another hour.

I will act now.

When I enter the market place I will say them and immediately confront my first prospect while the failure ponders yet his possibility of rebuff.

I will act now.

When I face a closed door I will say them and knock while the failure waits outside with fear and trepidation.

I will act now.

When I face temptation I will say them and immediately act to remove myself from evil.

I will act now.

When I am tempted to quit and begin again tomorrow I will say them and immediately act to consummate another sale.

I will act now.

Only action determines my value in the market place and to multiply my value I will multiply my actions.

I will walk where the failures fear to walk. I will work when the failure seeks rest. I will talk when the failure remains silent. I will call on ten who can buy my goods while the failure makes grand plans to call on one. I will say it is done before the failure says it is too late.

I will act now.

For now is all I have. Tomorrow is the day reserved for the labor of the lazy. I am not lazy. Tomorrow is the day when the evil become good. I am not evil. Tomorrow is the day when the weak become strong. I am not weak. Tomorrow is the day when failure will succeed. I am not a failure.

I will act now.

When the lion is hungry he eats. When the eagle has thirst he drinks. Lest they act, both will perish.

I hunger for success. I thirst for happiness and peace of mind. Lest I act I will perish in a life of failure, misery, and sleepless nights.

I will command, and I will obey mine own command.

I will act now.

Success will not wait. If I delay she will become betrothed to another and lost to me forever. This is the time. This is the place. I am the man.

I will act now.

The Scroll Marked X

*W*ho is of so little faith that in a moment of great disaster or heartbreak has not called to his God? Who has not cried out when confronted with danger, death, or mystery beyond his normal experience or comprehension? From where has this deep instinct come which escapes from the mouth of all living creatures in moments of peril? Move your hand in haste before another's eyes and his eyelids will blink. Tap another on his knee and his leg will jump. Confront another with dark horror and his mouth will say, "My God" from the same deep impulse.

My life need not be filled with religion in order for me to recognize this greatest mystery of nature. All creatures that walk the earth, including man, possess the instinct to cry for help. Why do we possess this instinct, this gift?

Are not our cries a form of prayer? Is it not incomprehensible in a world governed by nature's laws to give a lamb, or a mule, or a bird, or man the instinct to cry out for help lest some great mind has also provided that the cry should be heard by some superior power having the ability to hear and to answer our cry? Henceforth I will pray, but my cries for help will only be cries for guidance.

Never will I pray for the material things of the world. I am not calling to a servant to bring me food. I am not ordering an innkeeper to provide me with room. Never will I seek delivery of gold, love, good health, petty victories, fame, success, or happiness. Only for guidance will I pray, that I may be shown the way to acquire these things, and my prayer will always be answered.

The guidance I seek may come, or the guidance I seek may not come, but are not both of these an answer? If a child seeks bread from his father and it is not forthcoming has not the father answered?

I will pray for guidance, and I will pray as a salesman, in this manner—

Oh creator of all things, help me. For this day I go out into the world naked and alone, and without your hand to guide me I will

wander far from the path which leads to

success and happiness.

I ask not for gold or garments or even opportunities equal to my ability; instead, guide me so that I may acquire ability   equal to my opportunities.

You have taught the lion and the eagle how to hunt and prosper with teeth and claw. Teach me how to hunt with words and prosper with love so that I may be a lion among men and an eagle in the market place.

Help me to remain humble through obstacles and failures; yet hide not from mine eyes the prize that will come with victory.

Assign me tasks to which others have failed; yet guide me to pluck the seeds of success from their failures. Confront me with fears

that will temper my spirit; yet endow me
   with courage to laugh at my
               misgivings.

Spare me sufficient days to reach my
goals; yet help me to live this day as
         though it may be my last.

Guide me in my words that they may bear
fruit; yet silence me from gossip that
            none be maligned.

Discipline me in the habit of trying and
trying again; yet show me the way to make
use of the law of averages. Favor me
with alertness to recognize opportunity; yet
endow me with patience which will concen-
            trate my strength.

Bathe me in good habits that the bad ones
may drown; yet grant me compassion for

weaknesses in others. Suffer me to know that all things shall pass; yet help me to count my blessings of today.

Expose me to hate so it not be a stranger; yet fill my cup with love to turn strangers into friends.

But all these things be only if thy will. I am a small and a lonely grape clutching the vine yet thou hast made me different from all others. Verily, there must be a special place for me. Guide me. Help me. Show me the way.

Let me become all you planned for me when my seed was planted and selected by you to sprout in the vineyard of the world.

Help this humble salesman.
Guide me, God.

Closing Statement from Editor Brian Feinblum

Thank you for reading *The Ten Ancient Scrolls for Success*. If you would like to learn more about us, please read on.

Frederick Fell Publishing, established in 1943 in New York City originally as Fell Publishers, relocated to Hollywood, Florida in 1984. With over 1600 published titles, some of our more prestigious authors include the best-selling Og Mandino, Irving Wallace, Walter B. Gibson, Robert L. Shook, Alan Truscott, Jane Roberts and Lillian Roth.

We publish the following genres: **self-help, business, how-to, health, hobby, reference, new age, cookbooks, inspirational** and **spirituality.**

For a complete catalog, send a SASE with five $.37 postage stamps, and write to:

Frederick Fell Publishing, Inc.
2131 Hollywood Blvd.
Hollywood, FL 33020
Web: http://www.fellpub.com
E-mail: info@fellpub.com

THE GREATEST SALESMAN IN THE WORLD

Og Mandino

With over 14,000,000 copies sold, this is the best-selling inspirational and sales book in the world. This is the first book ever written by Og Mandino. It contains the Ten Greatest Scrolls For Success that motivate the reader to higher achievement.

"Every sales manager should read THE GREATEST SALESMAN IN THE WORLD. It is a book to keep at the bedside, or on the living room table—a book to dip into as needed, to browse in now and then, to enjoy in small stimulating portions..."
— **Lester J. Bradshaw, Jr., Former Dean, Dale Carnegie Institute of Effective Speaking & Human Relations**

★*108 pages* ★*$14.95* ★*Cloth* ★*ISBN:0-8119-0067-3*